The Reality
of
Our Sacred Human Nature

The Reality of Our Sacred Human Nature: Our Origins and Our Destiny

For more information, please write the author directly: sabilillah@aol.com

FIRST EDITION

ISBN: 978-1-945873-06-5

THE REALITY
OF
OUR SACRED HUMAN NATURE

Our Origins and Our Destiny

Imam Faheem Shuaibe

CONTENTS

*To my dedicated wife Yolanda Mahasin Shuaibe,
our beautiful children,
their offspring,
and to all of our future generations.*

PROLOGUE

AN IMMEASURABLE AND incalculable legacy and inheritance has come into the world and been left behind by Imam W. D. Mohammed (ra). The subject matter of this publication is grounded in one single comment from him. He said, "When you know these four things about anything then you know everything about that thing." He made these comments in a hotel discussion during one of his many visits somewhere in the country. I had the good fortune to be present with him at that time and during many of his travels. On this particular occasion, he was addressing commentary on the first three verses of the 87th Chapter of the Holy Qur'an, Sura Al-A'la.

When Imam Mohammed (ra) passed away in 2008, wonderings as to, "What are we going to do now?" reverberated throughout the length and breadth of this country amongst his followers, yet the vast quantity of inexhaustible wisdom that he left behind was yet to be appreciated.

As the sun rose from me on a world without the physical presence of the Imam, I began to pursue the question, "What was the most important Word of the Imam, if it was true that his mission was a mission of language?" In my analysis of that question, I found that words and concepts like human, human being, human nature, human destiny and human society were central to his mission. Indeed, one of the last titles he accepted for himself was "Muslim American Spokesman for Human Salvation." Consequently, understanding our common human origin, our common human existence and our common human destiny seemed, to me, to be the most important "Thing" to understand in this life.

So in light of the question, the answer, and the principles laid down by the Imam, I set about completing the book that is before you now. It holds the answer, and only Allah knows best, to the question "What is The Reality of Our Sacred Human Nature?" "What are the four things that we need to know about our "Self" so that we might "know everything about that thing"?

May Allah guide you to the best understanding of your "True Self."

Imam Faheem Shuaibe (2018)

INTRODUCTION

D UE TO THE abstract nature of the subject, the true
picture of this unseen reality must necessarily be
given in abstract language, that is, in figurative
speech and symbols. Our desire is to give the true science
(Haqqiqi-Reality) of the created self and nature. In order
to give or to attain the true perception of a thing, in
this case the created self, one must conceptualize it (i.e.,
identify its concrete model) in a figure, which accurately
describes its nature and function.

One of my sayings is that "You don't know the subject
until you know the object." In this instance, our objective
is to name the conceptualization in such a way that it
will convey an intimate familiarity with the subject's 4
Universal Descriptions as in 87: 1-3:

سَبِّحِ ٱسْمَ رَبِّكَ ٱلْأَعْلَى ۝

ٱلَّذِى خَلَقَ فَسَوَّىٰ ۝

وَٱلَّذِى قَدَّرَ فَهَدَىٰ ۝

- Glorify your Guardian Evolver, The Most High

- The one who gave everything its *[1]* Form and thereafter *[2]* A Place within the System

- The one who gave everything its *[3]* Potential for growth from simple to complex and thereafter its *[4]* Place in the Guidance of G_d

Imam Mohammed (ra) stated that "When you understand these **four things** about anything then you understand everything about that thing." The same 4 essentials found in 87: 1-3 are repeated, implicitly and explicitly, in this verse as well.

وَجَعَلَ فِيهَا رَوَاسِىَ مِن فَوْقِهَا وَبَارَكَ فِيهَا وَقَدَّرَ فِيهَآ أَقْوَاتَهَا فِىٓ أَرْبَعَةِ أَيَّامٍ سَوَآءً لِّلسَّآئِلِينَ ۝

41: 10 "And He *[1]* Created (Ja'ala synonymous in context for "Khalaqa") in the earth a basis for balance and stability from on High, and He put blessings in it and endowed it with immense potential *[3]* (Qadara) to nourish and sustain its life in four measures universally

[2] (Sowaa)—for the benefit of all enquirers *[4]* seeking guidance (Those who seek or are seeking Haada)."

Our methodology will be to inquire and extract the points of reference for these four important categories with reference to "The Reality of The Created Self."

THE SIGNIFICANCE OF MODELS

In science, models and analogies are used to tell a story about what happens in nature, in the material universe.

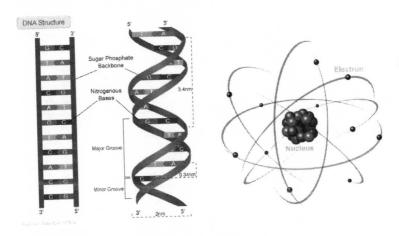

This is similar to what Allah does with revelation. He says that this is the way we stimulate curiosity in common people, but scientists already understand.

وَتِلْكَ ٱلْأَمْثَلُ نَضْرِبُهَا لِلنَّاسِ وَمَا يَعْقِلُهَا إِلَّا ٱلْعَلِمُونَ ۝

29:43 "And these examples We present to the common people, but none understand them except believing men of science."

In the Qur'an, Allah tells us the story of our original human nature through models, analogies, signs, and symbols in the form of words and word pictures and the like.

۞ إِنَّ ٱللَّهَ لَا يَسْتَحْىِۦٓ أَن يَضْرِبَ مَثَلًا مَّا بَعُوضَةً فَمَا فَوْقَهَا

2: 26. "Allah disdains not to use the similitude of things lowest as well as highest."

For example, when Abraham wanted to understand the Resurrection, which is quite abstract, Allah revealed the following:

وَإِذْ قَالَ إِبْرَهِيمُ رَبِّ أَرِنِي كَيْفَ تُحْىِ ٱلْمَوْتَىٰ قَالَ أَوَلَمْ تُؤْمِن قَالَ بَلَىٰ وَلَكِن
لِّيَطْمَئِنَّ قَلْبِى قَالَ فَخُذْ أَرْبَعَةً مِّنَ ٱلطَّيْرِ فَصُرْهُنَّ إِلَيْكَ ثُمَّ ٱجْعَلْ عَلَىٰ كُلِّ جَبَلٍ مِّنْهُنَّ
جُزْءًا ثُمَّ ٱدْعُهُنَّ يَأْتِينَكَ سَعْيًا وَٱعْلَمْ أَنَّ ٱللَّهَ عَزِيزٌ حَكِيمٌ ۝

2: 260. "Behold! Abraham said: "My Lord! show me how you give life to the dead. He said: "Do you not believe?" He said: "Yes! but to satisfy my own understanding." He said: "Take four birds; tame them to turn to you; put a portion of them on every hill and call to them; they will

6

come to you (flying) with speed. Then know that Allah is Exalted in Power Wise."

The Resurrection is a belief, a concept, and a reality that is abstract (i.e., not provable by pure reasoning to anyone who isn't already inclined to faith). However, this verse demonstrates to the believer that Allah gives to those with faith illustrations, models, and examples for such abstract matters in order to satisfy their hearts with understanding.

TRUTH AND REALITY ARE ULTIMATELY DISCERNED BY THE HEART

From this, we can understand that matters of the highest reality (Haqqiqi) are only discernable by the heart. Abraham is in many, many ways our model for the attainment of the highest possibilities for faith and perception.

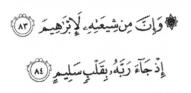

37: 83. "Verily among those who followed his Way was Abraham."

37: 84. "Behold He approached his Lord with a sound heart."

Allah tells us directly that it is "the heart that learns wisdom," "hears," or "sees" or is "blind."

أَفَلَمْ يَسِيرُوا فِي الْأَرْضِ فَتَكُونَ لَهُمْ قُلُوبٌ يَعْقِلُونَ بِهَا أَوْ ءَاذَانٌ يَسْمَعُونَ بِهَا فَإِنَّهَا لَا تَعْمَى الْأَبْصَٰرُ وَلَٰكِن تَعْمَى الْقُلُوبُ الَّتِي فِي الصُّدُورِ ﴿٤٦﴾

22: 46. "Do they not travel through the land so that their hearts may thus learn wisdom and their ears may thus learn to hear? Truly it is not their eyes that are blind but their hearts which are in their breasts."

Allah tells us directly that it is "the heart of the believer that is guided."

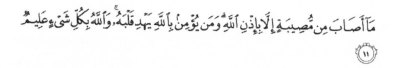

64: 11. "No kind of calamity can occur, except by the leave of Allah: and if any one believes in Allah, (Allah) guides his heart (aright): for Allah knows all things."

The Hadith of Prophet Muhammad(pbuh) also affirms that it is the heart of the believer that is guided and taught by parables, models, analogies, signs, symbols, and the like.

The hadith of Prophet Muhammad(pbuh) says, "Indeed, I saw in a dream as though Jibril was at my head and Mikail at my feet. One of them said to the other, "Indeed, he is asleep." The other replied, "Indeed, his eyes are asleep, but his heart is awake."

Then one of them said, "Indeed, there is a parable that applies to our companion, so tell him the parable." The other said, "Indeed, he is asleep." And the first replied, "Indeed, his eyes are asleep, but his heart is awake."

So, one of them said, "Listen, may your ear be able to hear; and understand, may your heart be able to understand; Indeed, the parable that applies to you and your people is that of a king who built a mansion, established in it a hall, set up in the hall a banquet, and then sent a messenger to invite people to his food. Some people answered the messenger, while others ignored him. Those who answered him entered the mansion and ate from the banquet, while those who ignored him neither entered the mansion nor ate from the banquet."

One of them said, "Interpret it for him so that he would understand it." But again, the other said, "Indeed, he is asleep." And the first replied, "Indeed, his eyes are alseep, but his heart is awake."

So, one of them said, "The king, then, is Allah, the mansion is Islam, the hall is Jannah (heaven), and you, O Muhammad, are the messenger; Whoever answers you will enter into Islam, and whoever enters into Islam will enter Jannah and eat from it. Therefore, whoever obeys Muhammad has surely obeyed Allah, and whoever disobeys Muhammad has surely disobeyed Allah. And Muhammad is a divider among the people."[1]

The refrain of this hadith is "Indeed, he is asleep." And the first replied, "Indeed, his eyes are asleep, but his heart is awake." So, it was his heart and not his conscious brain per se that was being taught. Likewise, with Yusuf (pbuh)

---

1 This hadith mirrors "The Kingdom of Heaven" parable in Luke 14: 15–24.

[HQ 12: 4], his heart received it even though his mind could not yet grasp its full import.

THE LANGUAGE OF THE HEART IS "FIGURATIVE SPEECH"

Long before the Prophets, there were seers and others and they saw that **the universe was really a reflection of what is in the soul.** That is why it is called, "Ghurrur." It is not real. It is real out there, but it is not real for the person who wants to understand that language and apply that language. You cannot do it. You are not supposed to apply it out there. You are supposed to apply it here, inside. So these seers were able to see into the nature for soul of man and see that **the language out there is really expressing the life in here.** God made that [the cosmos] to speak the language of the soul.[2]

The heart of the believer is the door of reception and perception of wisdom and guidance from Allah, especially of the abstract (i.e., higher order realities). The language of the heart is figurative speech (e.g., parables, allegories, metaphors, symbols, stories, illustrations, and the like).

---

2 Page 36 "Education: A Sacred Matter" Imam W. D. Mohammed (ra)Imam Al-Ghazzali(ra) identifies the Soul as having 4 components also Ruh, Nafs, Qalb and Aql. Spirit, Personality/Socialized Self, Heart and Intellect.

وَبَشِّرِ ٱلَّذِينَ ءَامَنُوا۟ وَعَمِلُوا۟ ٱلصَّـٰلِحَـٰتِ أَنَّ لَهُمْ جَنَّـٰتٍ تَجْرِى مِن تَحْتِهَا ٱلْأَنْهَـٰرُ
كُلَّمَا رُزِقُوا۟ مِنْهَا مِن ثَمَرَةٍ رِّزْقًا قَالُوا۟ هَـٰذَا ٱلَّذِى رُزِقْنَا مِن قَبْلُ وَأُتُوا۟ بِهِۦ
مُتَشَـٰبِهًا وَلَهُمْ فِيهَآ أَزْوَٰجٌ مُّطَهَّرَةٌ وَهُمْ فِيهَا خَـٰلِدُونَ ﴿٢٥﴾

2: 25. "But give glad tidings to those who believe and work righteousness that their portion is Gardens beneath which rivers flow. Every time they are fed with fruits therefrom they say: "Why this is what we were fed with before" for they are given things in similitude; and they have therein companions (pure and holy); and they abide therein (forever)."

The *Mutashabi-han* of this verse shows that in the end, all that the true believer has been given of good in this life is only a "reflection, symbol and a similitude, and the likeness" of the highest realities. Furthermore, the verb form of this term (Form VIII) makes it clear that it was received internally. Indeed, the reality was grasped by the believers who had reconciled the nature of this material world to their original nature by what they "8"

Imam Mohammed (ra) has provided a concrete articulation that explains the term *Amthal*.

A term that is often translated in the Holy Qur'an as "similitudes." He said, "When the Qur'an speaks of Amthal (similitudes) it means Allah gives us a picture (i.e., model) referring to the real thing (Haqqiqi) that he wants to talk to us about. He gives us something (concrete) that we can visualize

11

first. In English 102, it's called a Metaphor. It is the symbolic picture (i.e., model) holding or enshrouding the real thing that G'd wants us to have or that he wants to reach us with.[3]

Jeffrey Burton Russell writes,

> The reality of G'd is so much greater and broader then we can begin to understand that G'd is obliged to speak to us in metaphor and analogy. The Quran is absolutely true but the truth that it gives us, holy as it is, can be only a pale shadow of the truth that exist in the "mind of G'd." The Quran's revelation is complete so far as human understanding is able to grasp but it is limited by the inadequacies of human speech and human concepts.

An analogy or a similitude is a mental map and an objectification of an intangible reality. We use analogies, metaphors, stories, and the like to describe, explain, or understand abstract and complicated concepts, ideas, or principles. Allah has revealed the truth, reality, and science of our created self and nature. He has done so by using the plain and the abstract language of the Qur'anic Arabic Prophetic figures and personalities as well as figurative speech, analogies, metaphors, and stories in scripture. Consequently, insha'Allah, we intend to make explicit what Allah has revealed about the reality of the created self. We will use, as a working tool throughout, Imam Mohammed's statement:

---

3 Imam Mohammed Raleigh, N. C. June 17, 2007.

"The Quran uses figurative expression, figurative speech, abstract symbols (Ayah/Signs/Parables) to address what is actual and what is scientific, what is very real."[4]

This statement is supported by the Holy Quran 29: 43.

وَتِلْكَ ٱلْأَمْثَـٰلُ نَضْرِبُهَا لِلنَّاسِ وَمَا يَعْقِلُهَآ إِلَّا ٱلْعَـٰلِمُونَ ۝

"And such are the figurative expressions We compose for the benefit of civilized human beings, and none intellectually grasp these except men at the height of faith and science."

Again, this concept is addressed in 25: 33:

وَلَا يَأْتُونَكَ بِمَثَلٍ إِلَّا جِئْنَـٰكَ بِٱلْحَقِّ وَأَحْسَنَ تَفْسِيرًا ۝

"There is no figurative expression, analogy or argument they can bring you but that we give you the truth and reality of it and the best explanation."

Consequently, the best, true and real (Haqqiqi) perception of the reality of the created self will be gained by (1) reading or extracting the insights from what Allah has revealed about it in the Holy Qur'an, (2) reading or extracting the insights from what Prophet Muhammad (pbuh) has articulated about it, and (3) studying those two sources through the lens of the methodology of Imam Mohammed (ra), insha'Allah. Allah knows best.

---

4 12-28-80 Imam Warith Deen Muhammad National Broadcast.

The ultimate significance of having this complete perception of the reality of the created self is that "having it will enable us to follow the perfect steps of logic"[5] to our full development in this world and, thereby, "qualify for entrance into the best life in the next."[6] And Allah knows best.

---

5 Imam Mohammed (ra) "Family and Progress" Newark, NJ 7/30/95.
6 ibid.

SECTION 1:
KHALAQA

WHAT IS THE FORM
OF THE HUMAN BEING?

THE OBJECTIVE OF this section is to give a clear perception of the form and nature of our humanity, which is our created self and nature. This section will attempt to answer the question: What is the reality of our created self and nature?[7] The reality of our created self and nature is both abstract and concrete.

The Abstract Reality of the Human Being

The abstract reality of our created self and nature is virtue and excellence. This meaning is communicated in the verse:

$$\text{لَقَدْ خَلَقْنَا ٱلْإِنسَٰنَ فِىٓ أَحْسَنِ تَقْوِيمٍ ﴿٤﴾}$$

95: 4. "We have indeed created man in the best of molds."

---

7 The name, the sign and/or the expression that holds the secret science (revelation) of our "Created Self and Nature."

Grammatically, the opening particle of the verse is called *Jawwabul-Qasim*; it's the answer to the oath that Allah himself made in the previous verses. Sayyid Abu Ala Maududi (ra) explains this in his tafsir of the verse as follows:

> This is the truth for which the oath has been sworn by the lands of the fig and the olive (i.e. Syria and Palestine) and Mt. Sinai and Makkah, the city of peace. Man's having been created in the most excellent of molds means that he has been given the finest body which no other living being has been given, and he has been blessed with the noblest faculties of thought, knowledge and intellect which no other creature has been blessed with.[8]

The phrase that is translated here as "The Best of Molds" is called an *Idaafa*, a genitive or possessive-construct phrase, which can also be translated as "The Mold of Excellence." The phrase contains two nouns related to each other in such a way that, when read in Arabic, the first term is possessed by the second term. Additionally, the single object actually being labeled by the phrase is the first term. So, in this construction, "The Mold of Excellence," "The Mold" is what is emphasized. For example, a "Chalice of Gold" is describing the "Chalice" and stating that its essential makeup is "Gold." Likewise, "The Mold of Excellence" means that the essential makeup of "The Mold" is "Excellence."

---

8 Tafheemul Quran 95: 4, footnote 3.

Another way of reading the phrase is in an "'s" form, which is also the possessive form. As awkward as it might be, the phrase would be stated as "The Excellence's Mold." In either reading, what is being identified is "The Mold" and that "The Mold" is always possessed in its nature by excellence as well as beauty.

So, the highest reference of the verse is to our abstract form, the non-material structure. *Akhlaq*, which means "character" is derived from the term, *Khalaqa*. Thus, a person of excellent character is a person of virtue. Imam Mohammed (ra) has championed the call back to that original excellence. He said,

> "What we perhaps need more than anything else in this world today is the innocence that G'd created us with and that all of us are born with."[9]

"The Mold" also refers to the "concrete form," the human anatomy, as understood from the same term *Khalaqa* (he formed) in the verse.[10] Imam Mohammed addressed this aspect of the verse as follows:

> . . . that progression (95: 1-3), is followed by *"Laqad khalaqnaal insaana fee ahsani taqweem."* 'indeed, 'it's a strong emphasis here, stronger than *"inna."* *"Laqad"*, indeed, we created the human in the best of molds'" That's how it's translated, "in the best of molds." *"Fee ahsani taqweem."* *"Taqweem"* is from

---

9   01-14-05_Bridging Diversity, Communities of Health, Hope and the Human Spirit (Reflections for the New Year 2005).
10   The Golden Ratio material regarding how human beings perceive "Beauty" could be added here.

"qaum," from *"qama,"* "stood up, to stand." *"Fee ahsani taqweem,"* in the best of molds, in the best of postures." Couldn't we say that? Because it comes from *"qama."* "to stand"; in the best of postures, or in the best of molds.[11]

This truth that Allah "Swears by" is also borne out by the scientific reality of human anatomical structure as compared to all other forms of organic life. According to an article on the website, Scitable: A Collaborative Learning Space for Science:

What do a human, a rose, and a bacterium have in common? Each of these things—along with every other organism on Earth—contains the molecular instructions for life, called deoxyribonucleic acid or DNA. Encoded within this DNA are the directions for traits as diverse as the color of a person's eyes, the scent of a rose, and the way in which bacteria infect a lung cell.

DNA is found in nearly all living cells . . . Human DNA is housed within the nucleus . . . Although each organism's DNA is unique, all DNA is composed of the same nitrogen-based molecules. So how does DNA differ from organism to organism? It is simply the order in which these smaller molecules are arranged that differs among individuals. In turn, this pattern of arrangement ultimately determines each organism's unique characteristics, thanks to another set of molecules

11 Ramadan Imams' Session, Athens, Georgia, February 25, 1995.

that "read" the pattern and stimulate the chemical and physical processes it calls for.[12]

The last statement is the key. That is, while human beings share the nitrogen-based molecules of DNA with all other forms of life, *"the mold and structure"* of the human being is the most excellent of them all. And *this pattern is based on* "the arrangement of smaller molecules" which is determined by another set of molecules that "read" the pattern and stimulate the chemical and physical processes it calls for."

The big and main question is this: Who decides the pattern that is called forth as the "final design and construction"? It is Allah who "chose the molecules and the reading" and the chemical and physical processes that give the final outcome, which distinguishes the human being in its excellent anatomical, biological mold and structure. The Will of Allah in matter is executed in these processes. We are Allah's artistry and his most excellent design. As he says directly:

> 40: 64 ". . . It is Allah Who has . . . given you shapes and made your shapes beautiful . . ."

Both readings express the unique quality of the original human nature (abstract) and the human form (concrete) that Allah has created for us as human beings. The excellence of our original nature is that it entails all excellent human qualities and virtues conceived and brought into

---

12 http://www.nature.com/scitable/topicpage/
dna-is-a-structure-that-encodes-biological-6493050.

existence by Allah, alone. For example, honesty, trust, integrity, modesty, courage, curiosity, compassion, love, charity, the devotional nature to serve and worship Allah are all endowments from Allah to our original human nature. Furthermore, because we are specially designed by the creator of the skies and the earth with this unique essence, every human being, is by nature an Immaculate Conception.

Imam Mohammed(ra) states,

> Jesus represents a sign for man to reconcile his life again with nature as Adam did. He is the second Adam, Jesus Christ. Reconcile your life again with the nature created by G_d and then you will find patterns for your thinking that will bring you to the great destination that God wants you to reach for your capacity and your potential inside of you.[13]

Additionally, Imam Mohammed (ra) said,

> We have to stop telling people that man is born in sin. We have to separate the allegory from the real in the Bible and let the people know that the Immaculate Conception is not the flesh born body (Of Jesus Christ). The thing that is immaculate is the will in the individual to submit to the Will of G-d. That's the Immaculate Conception.[14]

---

13 "Education: A Sacred Matter" Imam W. D. Mohammed(ra) Page 117
14 3-19-78 Imam W. D. M on Excellence (Venue of the speech unknown).

This accords with what has been stated about our original human nature. The highest of those excellent human qualities and high human virtues is "the will to submit to the Will of G-d." This is why Jesus Christ (pbuh) is a symbol of our original human nature created by Allah, alone.[15]

Some of the many definitions of *Khalaqa* are:

> To have an innate/natural disposition/temperament/ quality.
>
> To originate according to a pattern or model which one has devised.
>
> To bring into existence from a state of non-existence.
>
> To be complete or perfect in respect of make or proportion.

With reference to our essential and original existence, *khalaqa* is synonymous with Fitrah, which is the original human nature as conceived for human beings by Allah in a specific form. In Sura 30: 30, these two terms define each other as well as our Deen (religion).

فَأَقِمْ وَجْهَكَ لِلدِّينِ حَنِيفًا فِطْرَتَ ٱللَّهِ ٱلَّتِي فَطَرَ ٱلنَّاسَ عَلَيْهَا لَا تَبْدِيلَ لِخَلْقِ ٱللَّهِ ذَٰلِكَ ٱلدِّينُ ٱلْقَيِّمُ وَلَٰكِنَّ أَكْثَرَ ٱلنَّاسِ لَا يَعْلَمُونَ ﴿٣٠﴾

---

15 Thus, putting aside what is false about the Crucifixion, it can be read as the ultimate willingness in human nature to die according to Allah's Will. See Supplement (F) Imam Mohammed's(ra) tafseer on the Crucifixion and Holy Quran 3: 102.

Sahih International: So, direct your face toward the religion, inclining to truth. [Adhere to] the Fitrah of Allah upon which He has created [all] people. No change should there be in the creation of Allah. That is the correct religion, but most of the people do not know.

This verse expresses that our Deen, our Fitrah,[16] and our Khalq are one. It reveals that our human form (abstract and concrete) is the embodiment/manifestation of Allah's conception of our Humanity [Fitrah]. Also, the verse begins and ends by saying be committed to "it" [the Deen] then describing "it" and defining "the Deen as the Fitrah of Allah" and commanding us not to change "it" and thus defining "the Deen and the Fitrah of Allah" as the Khalq.

So, the first form (Khalq), though invisible to our physical eye, is the original essence of our unique human creation that Allah, alone, and no other, originally conceived as excellent human qualities and human virtues, both concrete and abstract.

SO, WHERE DO WE BEGIN?

As we stated earlier, we intend to make explicit what Allah has revealed about the reality of the created self by using, as a principle, Imam Mohammed's(ra) statement:

The Quran uses figurative expression, figurative speech, abstract symbols (Ayah/Signs/Parables) to

---

16 The unprecedented conception/idea of humanity that is Allah's alone.

address what is actual and what is scientific, what is very real.[17]

Allah reveals the truth and the reality of our created self in the meanings found in the figurative expressions, figurative speech, abstract symbols in his revelation, and the like. By the permission of Allah, through the "Objects, substances, qualities and circumstances" presented as the story of our "Genesis," depicted in Allah's revelation about that event and in the reports of Prophet Muhammad (pbuh) about it, we can learn about the reality of the created self.

Our human nature (original humanity) doesn't begin on earth. It was originated (Fitrah) by Allah and put into matter (Ja'ala/Khalaqa) then evolved out of the matter to come into its "earthly-life" existence in a human body and grow to express its endowment of excellent qualities through social interaction.

The evidence that our human origin wasn't and isn't on the Earth is in Allah's revelation and can be read from the story of our expulsion from the realm of our original creation after Adam and his wife were seduced by Satan.

فَأَزَلَّهُمَا ٱلشَّيْطَانُ عَنْهَا فَأَخْرَجَهُمَا مِمَّا كَانَا فِيهِ وَقُلْنَا ٱهْبِطُوا بَعْضُكُمْ لِبَعْضٍ عَدُوٌّ وَلَكُمْ فِى ٱلْأَرْضِ مُسْتَقَرٌّ وَمَتَٰعٌ إِلَىٰ حِينٍ ﴿٣٦﴾

2: 36 "... We said: "Get ye down, all, with enmity between yourselves.[18] On earth will be your dwelling-place and your means of livelihood – for a time."

17 Imam Mohammed Raleigh, N. C. June 17, 2007.
18 This can be illustrated by the symmetry of our human form which, in large part, is due to the natural opposition of

This is figurative expression, figurative speech, by which Allah is telling us that, as an original creation, the beginning of our existence is/was "like this story." Since the revelation is about "this life" (i.e., for "we the living"), this story is telling us about our existence as sentient, conscious beings in this life. This then refers to a state of original innocence that was changed to become a state less than innocent during our life in this world. There was a time in our lives "here and now" when we were "without guile," but then we are caused to become "guilty" of sin [disobedient].

The source of our "guile-lessness" was/is our original human nature conforming to the Will of Allah. The source of our guilt was/is accepting the invitation to disobey the Will of Allah. Consequently, the Paradise/the Higher State was/is our original state of obedience and the resulting peaceful condition The Earth/the Lower State (was/is our human state where we learn/are taught, through trial and error and the guidance of Allah, how to return consciously to our original state of obedience and the resulting peaceful condition). So, as a conception of Allah, alone, our human origin was/is above and beyond the earthly domain. Our original humanity, which is distinct from our physical anatomy, is, ontologically speaking, from the highest domain of created reality.

When we apply Imam Mohammed's maxim (i.e., "figurative expression in scripture is addressing something that is scientific, actual, and very real") to the imagery of coming from a "very high place," it communicates that our original nature is constituted of all excellent human

---

"antagonistic pairs of muscles."

qualities and all high human virtues and more, as conceived and brought into existence by Allah, alone. Whenever we act in ways contrary to those excellences, we are acting in our fallen state. (HQ 95: 1-8)

Uppermost of those excellent human qualities and virtues is obedience to Allah.

وَمَا خَلَقْتُ الْجِنَّ وَالْإِنسَ إِلَّا لِيَعْبُدُونِ ﴿٥٦﴾

"And I did not create the jinn and mankind except to worship Me." (**Sahih International**: 51: 56)

It is in our nature to obey Allah just as "the Sun and the Moon follows courses computed for them" (Sura 55: 5). It is in that state and condition of obedience to Allah's Will that our nature was originated (Sura 30: 30).[19] As Imam Mohammed (ra) has explained, "Eidul-Fitrah" is a memorial of that state, the condition and the means of our "return to our original nature."

> The Eidul-Fitrah itself . . . is not just a holiday in the sense that we understand holidays in the western world. It doesn't just celebrate something empty, something without meaning something playful or joyful. It celebrates that that brings the human being the greatest joy. The greatest joy comes when

---

19 Imam Mohammed says, "Three (3) equals Man's developmental nature." He also states that "10 is Conscious." So, 30 would mean becoming conscious in or of your developmental nature. In turn, 30: 30 would carry the same meaning as 71: 17.

the human being's life is reconciled with his nature as Allah intended.[20]

This relationship of the abstract original life to our concrete bodies is well illustrated by the premise of the movie, *The Odd Life of Timothy Green*. Here is the plot given with marketing the movie:

> Timothy isn't born, and he isn't adopted. He seems to have grown in the garden. The movie very wisely makes no attempt to explain how this happened. His new parents have tried everything to conceive a child of their own, and one desperate night, they open a bottle of red wine and start making a list of the things their perfect child should have. They put the list in a box and bury it in their garden, and after a torrential downpour and a lightning storm—why, there's Timothy, covered with wet earth and with leaves growing from his legs.

Timothy came into existence in the garden, born of the attributes of excellence written on a list, by the movie's starring man and woman. Their list is analogous to the Fitrah—the original nature of the human being, which is comprised of the excellent masculine attributes and the excellent feminine attributes, as conceived by Allah before those attributes were placed in matter and then came into the human anatomy.

---

20 Imam Warith Deen Mohammed, Oakland, Ca. August 1, 1981.

To conceptualize this as a "pre-body" or non-material existence, just imagine the aggregate of all possible human virtues and excellences without a body. Consider that the aggregation of human virtues and excellences, *in toto*, reflects the "immaculate conception," our original human nature—our Fitrah as conceived by Allah, alone, in his transcendent realm, before those human virtues and excellences were embedded in matter and embodied in a human anatomy. That is *Nafsun Wahidah*.

Nafsun Wahidah

This "pre-body," abstract state of our original nature is what Allah reveals as the *Nafsun Wahidah* in Sura 4: 1 in the Holy Quran:

يَٰٓأَيُّهَا ٱلنَّاسُ ٱتَّقُوا۟ رَبَّكُمُ ٱلَّذِى خَلَقَكُم مِّن نَّفْسٍ وَٰحِدَةٍ وَخَلَقَ مِنْهَا زَوْجَهَا وَبَثَّ مِنْهُمَا رِجَالًا كَثِيرًا وَنِسَآءً وَٱتَّقُوا۟ ٱللَّهَ ٱلَّذِى تَسَآءَلُونَ بِهِۦ وَٱلْأَرْحَامَ إِنَّ ٱللَّهَ كَانَ عَلَيْكُمْ رَقِيبًا ﴿١﴾

4: 1 "O mankind, be regardful of your Guardian Evolver, who created you from one soul and created from it its mate and dispersed from both of them many men and women. And fear Allah, through whom you ask one another, and the wombs. Indeed, Allah is ever, over you, an Observer.

O mankind, be regardful of your Guardian Evolver, who created you {i.e., [Kum] – All existing human beings are being addressed, by Allah, about our "origin"} **from ONE SOUL** [*A synonym for Fitrah – The original Masculine and Feminine Potential in one unitary pre-anatomical existence*] **and created from it its mate** [*The Male and Female Anatomy*] **and from the two of them** {*The Nature and The*

29

Form} spread many men and women. And be regardful of Allah, whom you mutually implore, and be regardful of the wombs. Indeed, Allah is ever, over you, an Observer."

Essentially, this verse is pointing to the origins of our human nature and the subsequent creation of our human bodies. It addresses the infusion of our nature into our human bodies. So, in reality (Haqq), our individuality and separateness are only "apparent." Our separateness from each other is only an illusion (ghurrur). As Allah says, "And your creation or your resurrection is in no wise but as a Single Soul (Nafsin Wahidatin)."[21]

This process and feature of our human existence is restated explicitly in the Holy Quran chapter 23 verses 12 through 14.

23: 12. "Man We did create from a quintessence (of clay);

13. Then We placed him as (a drop of) sperm in a place of rest firmly fixed;

14. Then We made the sperm into a clot of congealed blood; then of that clot We made a (foetus) lump; then We made out of that lump bones and clothed the bones with flesh; then We developed out of it another creature: so blessed be Allah the Best to create!

This set of verses delineates the development of the human body from substance in matter to inception to full maturity and its final culmination in a connected, but

---

21   31: 28

distinct phenomena that the Qur'an identifies as "Another Creation."[22] The first sections of 23: 12-14, namely verses 12 and 13, define "the creation of our human bodies." The final statement in verse 14 defines "the creation of our 'Individual Souls' from Adam: First Soul; Great Soul (Nafsin Wahidatin/Fitrah)."

The statement, "Dispersed from both of them countless men and women," speaks to the propagation and the varieties and distinctions that we attain as human beings by virtue of the dynamic relationships among "multiple dualities":

> The Duality of Fitrah (Nature) and Khalaqa (Form)
>
> The Duality of Soul and Body
>
> The Duality of Female and Male
>
> The Duality of Nature [Genetics] and Nurture [Environment]

THE EARTH IS THE HUMAN BODY

It is not coincidental that the topsoil of the earth is called humus. And that the Bible and the Holy Quran speak of Adam as being made from the earth. As I was writing this section, I received a call from my wife. She began to explain to me that our daughter said to her that for some strange reason, she had been having a craving for dirt. She also began to have a craving for chalk. Being concerned

---

22 It's what science would call and "An **epiphenomenon** (plural: **epiphenomena**): a secondary phenomenon that occurs alongside or in parallel to a primary phenomenon. The word has two senses,[1] [2] one that connotes known causation and one that connotes absence of causation or reservation of judgment about it.[1][2]

about these strange cravings [and I might add never acting upon them], she "Googled" the question: "What is the cause of craving for dirt?" The reply that she got from her search was that it is an indication that the body is suffering a severe deficiency in iron or magnesium. In fact, my daughter had been taking a regular regimen of magnesium and iron, but her supply had just run out. So, when she finally did get a resupply of iron and magnesium and took some, the cravings immediately went away. Why? Because the body wants and needs what it is. The earth, literally and figuratively, is the human body.

When Allah conceived and created our original human nature (Fitrah), he never intended for it to remain without a physical body (Khalaqa). That claim is easily derived from Allah's statement in Sura 2 Ayah 30:

$$\text{وَإِذْ قَالَ رَبُّكَ لِلْمَلَٰٓئِكَةِ إِنِّي جَاعِلٌ فِي ٱلْأَرْضِ خَلِيفَةً ۖ قَالُوٓاْ أَتَجْعَلُ فِيهَا مَن}$$
$$\text{يُفْسِدُ فِيهَا وَيَسْفِكُ ٱلدِّمَآءَ وَنَحْنُ نُسَبِّحُ بِحَمْدِكَ وَنُقَدِّسُ لَكَ ۖ قَالَ إِنِّيٓ أَعْلَمُ مَا}$$
$$\text{لَا تَعْلَمُونَ ﴿٣٠﴾}$$

"Behold, your Lord said to the angels: "I am making in earth a Khalifah.""

From this statement, it is clear that even before there was human existence on earth, Allah intended that Adam would be placed "in the earth."[23] Why? The physical human form is necessary because our original human nature can

---

23 "...God raises us up. He creates us in this earth. Our physical essences are of this creation, of this earth--in this physical universe. Our conscience is born of this physical environment, this natural environment. And God has already set the pattern of that growth, that progress, in the physical matter that we are from--- and, also,

only function in a form fit for its expression on earth (i.e., human anatomy). Also our original human nature can only evolve in a forum (i.e., human society) suited to cultivate its virtues and excellences. Thus, when we apply Imam Mohammed's maxim: "Figurative Expression in scripture is addressing something that is scientific, actual and very real."– to "On earth will be your place of establishment to fulfill your purpose and your means of enjoyment of good and useful things – for a time."

(HQ 2: 36), we can draw two meaningful premises to support our thesis.

1. That "the earth is a symbol for "our human anatomy."[24]

2. That "the earth" is also a symbol for "social situations."

This means that that original human nature, which is nonphysical and abstract, yet most real, is going to be made concrete in the human anatomy and then evolved into a society of people. The existence of this *non-corporeal*

---

in our biology, and, also, in the spiritual makeup [Fitrah/Adam] that lives in this biology…

The physical matter has the pattern [Fitrah/Adam]. That pattern [Fitrah/Adam] comes into me and I become a living being. (See 23: 12-14) That pattern [Fitrah/Adam] is now in me as a physical living [human] being. The pattern [Fitrah/Adam] is in my physiology, When it reaches my mental makeup, my conscience. Then it begins to set the pattern of my conscience (i.e., it becomes my conscience). God has designed all of this!! And it brings us up step by step." Imam Mohammed(ra) "Growth of Human Consciousness"
24   Imam Mohammed's Address on "The Role of Khalifah in the Moral Life" addresses the role of the body in moral guidance. That nature is established in the body and the societal demands cultivate its vast potential

state in transit" is confirmed in the Hadith of the Prophet (pbuh), which follows.

Abu Huraira narrated: "They said: 'O Messenger of Allah! When was the Prophethood established for you?' He said: 'While Adam was between[25] soul and body." This means that there was a time when Adam was between abstract and concrete—between "Fitrah {being originated} and Khalaqa {being formed}."

According to the hadith, these virtues and excellences were placed in the root nature, the Fitrah, of the human being. Hudhaifah, may Allah be pleased with him, reported:

> Allah's Messenger (may peace be upon him) . . . He told us: was placed in the nature of people, then the Qur'an was revealed and they learnt from the Qur'an and they learnt from My Sunnah.[26]

Therefore, ontologically speaking, there was a transitional state wherein "Adam" existed but not in or as a body. By his transcendent power, Allah created our original humanity (Fitrah; non-corporeal), from his conception of excellent human qualities and high human virtues[27] then placed in the matter that became our bodies.

Imam Mohammed(ra) has also given us a practical inter-pretation of this reality of the human being's creation in the heavens and then being placed in the earth. He says

---

25 i.e., in transition from . . . abstract to concrete.
26 Deenul Fitrah.
27 For example, thinking of the scope of such values, "What does Allah mean by "Justice or Love or Forgiveness or Patience or Courage or Mercy, etc." Well, whatever he meant that is what he put in our original nature.

The explanation for the belief that we had a creation in the heavens before down here is this – the heavens are symbolic of the obedience to God that created it. This is why Allah points to the obedience that you see in the heavens – "see how the sun and the moon follow courses computed for them." So, being created in the heavens means that we were once created with that heavenly obedience and then our minds came on or was opened on the world down here and the world down here eventually takes our nature, our obedience, away from the nature or the heavenly obedience that God created in us from the beginning. So that's what is meant by "we were first made in the heavens and then in the earth."[28]

Since original humanity is abstract and not concrete, "Adam," in scripture, should be read as a personification of the original humanity of all men and women and not as one biological male. This same message of "Spirit/Nature before Body/Form" is more allegorically stated in the Bible. Imam Mohammed has said, "We have to separate the allegory from the real in the Bible." The Bible says, "Then the LORD God said, "It is not good for the man to be alone; I will make him a helper suitable for him."[29]

When we conceptualize Adam as the personification of the original human nature (abstract) and "His Mate [in the Holy Qur'an]/Eve [in the Bible]" as both the human anatomy and the society (concrete), we can see that [with

28 Imam's Newark, NJ address 7/30/95.
29 Genesis 2: 18; KJV says "Helpmeet"; See Holy Qur'an "Mates of like nature" 4: 1; 30:21.

qualification] Adam and Eve are used in the Bible to address the same sacred matter[30] that is addressed in the Holy Quran 4: 1; 30:30 as the truth about original human nature.

The revelation in this verse of Genesis is that the original human nature must have a mate in order to grow. The mate of our original human nature is, first, the universal system of creation itself, and second, the human anatomy and society.[31] In Gen. 5:1, the Bible speaks of the shared origin of human nature for both males and females under one name *Adam*. It says,

This is the book of the generations of Adam. In the day that God created man, in the likeness[32] of God made he him; Male and female created he them; and blessed them, and called their name Adam, in the day when they were created.

The duality of our original nature is also expressed in Surah 4 Ayah 1

يَٰٓأَيُّهَا ٱلنَّاسُ ٱتَّقُوا۟ رَبَّكُمُ ٱلَّذِى خَلَقَكُم مِّن نَّفْسٍ وَٰحِدَةٍ وَخَلَقَ مِنْهَا زَوْجَهَا وَبَثَّ مِنْهُمَا رِجَالًا كَثِيرًا وَنِسَآءً ۚ وَٱتَّقُوا۟ ٱللَّهَ ٱلَّذِى تَسَآءَلُونَ بِهِۦ وَٱلْأَرْحَامَ ۚ إِنَّ ٱللَّهَ كَانَ عَلَيْكُمْ رَقِيبًا ﴿١﴾

---

30 "Abstract/Concrete"; "Soul/Body"; "Nature/Form" of the Human Being.
31 Imam Mohammed also invites us to recognize the Universe as our mate as well. Page 40 of 49 Ramadan Session 2002.
32 A nature comprised of the human reflections of Allah's attributes. To take "Created in the image of G'd," anthropomorphically would mean that G'd is androgynous which is, of course, absurd. "Created in the image of G'd," is speaking of the practical indiscernible, invisible, and abstract quality of human nature.

"O mankind, be regardful of your Guardian Evolver, who created you from one soul and created from it its mate and dispersed from both of them many men and women. And be regardful of Allah, whom you mutually implore, and of the wombs. Indeed, Allah is ever, over you, an Observer."

Our original conception by Allah, under the name *Adam* and in the expression *Nafsun Wahidah*, entails all the excellent human qualities and all the human virtues of the masculine and the feminine, before they were endowed to our male and female anatomies. Thus, according to the Bible and the Holy Quran, Adam is not a single biological male. He (It) is the scripture's personification of "the Human Soul," the abstract, nonphysical original humanity of both males and females created by Allah. Allah reveals the nature of this "duality in reality" in the Holy Quran. He says,

13: 3 ". . . and fruit of every kind He made in pairs, two and two"

The implication of this verse is that Allah creates "pairs of pairs." For our current reference, it means that the "two and two" entail an "abstract pair" and a "concrete pair."

The abstract pair is the Fitrah/original nature (nonphysical) conceived by Allah of masculine and feminine excellence and virtue in all human beings. The concrete pair is the *Khalaqa/*the anatomy (physical biology) of the male and the female designed by Allah to give expression to the (nonphysical essence) of masculine and feminine excellence and virtue.

37

The statement in Sura 4 Ayah 1, "created from it, its mate," is a reference to the male and female biological forms which have been created with the structures and capacities suited to express their respective excellent human qualities and human virtues in society as man and woman. The male body is the mate for the expression of the masculine excellences and virtues and the female body is the mate for the expression of the feminine excellences and virtues. This is also a meaning of "He made in pairs, two and two."

> The human being has two fundamental principles operating in him and even more. One inspires him to improve his ability to cultivate the material world and the other inspires him to improve his ability to cultivate the human spirituality.
>
> One is of the physical creation and the other is inspired by the nature that is given to him before even the physical appetite was there—given to him by G'd, his Creator—the nature to rise above even his first form.[33]

Therefore, according to the Bible and the Holy Quran, it's very clear that Adam is not a single biological male. He is scripture's personification of the metaphysical human soul, the original human nature—humanity. Adam is a type for the original form and nature of the male and the female as created by Allah. So, the first and original form, *Khalaqa*, of our sacred human nature is all the excellent human qualities and all the human virtues of the masculine and the feminine, as conceived by Allah before they were endowed to our male and female anatomies.

33 02-09-79_The Shackles of Slavery

SECTION 2:
SOWAA

WHAT IS THE PLACE OF THE ORIGINAL HUMAN NATURE IN THE TOTAL SCHEME OF CREATION?

THE OBJECTIVE OF this section is to give a clear perception of the place of the original form and nature of the human being (Adam) in the total scheme of creation. The intent is to view the place of our original form and nature in the totality of creation. The object is to know where the human being is to be properly located as a category of existence relative to the universe at large and relative to all life on earth.

As a point of interest, it is noteworthy to consider the findings of Mr. Nassim Haramain.[34] He found that cosmically and mathematically speaking, the human being is in the middle of the universe. Using relativistic equations, his research team plotted the energy levels and

---
34   Nassim Haramain's "Black Whole" video.

radius of different phenomena in creation from the largest to smallest. When these scientific measurements were plotted on a graph, the human being plotted at the exact mid-point between the largest and the smallest dimensions of the known creation.

The revealed truth is that the original form and nature of humanity is distinct from all other forms of life. It is the human beings' unique endowments, in form and nature, which give the human being this unique "place within the total system of creation." In fact, Imam Mohammed says, "Our own [human] existence explains the existence of everything else."[35] Consider this statement:

> For the human being, life is the life of our intellect. For the animal, life is the life of the biology. If we can see all living things as one life and the human being representing the head of that life, then it makes sense that G'd evolves the head from the simplest form. . . . (It makes sense) that G'd evolves man, the human from the simplest form. Am I giving support to Darwin? No. Allah says that He created us from a clot, alaq, and He says even less than that, He says, (from) water. And He says even less than that, lifeless, clinging clay, or dust. He said He created us from that. So He's saying he created us from the most insignificant, from the simplest form of matter and evolved us to this highly complex machine we call the human person, the human being.

---

35 Imam Mohammed (ra) "Family and Progress," Newark, NJ 7/30/95.

So I repeat, that if we understand that life is one and that G'd has gradually evolved that life and the final stage of that life (The Human Being) is able to think free, question, imagine, make improvements, recreate, and appreciate the G'd that designed all this,[36] then G'd is justified in making those elementary (evolutionary) steps that lead to the final step." [37]

The place of the original human nature in the total system of creation is as the, metaphorical head on the body of the universe. Imam Mohammed (ra) said, "If Allah had stopped the creation short of man, then it wouldn't make sense. Just like if he would have stopped the creation of the body short of a head, and just left a neck up their alive, and no head; neck with no head. if G'd had stopped short of us, and left the universe just like that, nothing but a corpse with no head on it, that's how I would see the universe."[38]

What gives the original human nature its special place within the total system of creation? Imam Mohammed (ra) says,

The human did not receive life by material activity. The human received the life by the . . . (Allah)

---

36 Tie this reference to Dr. Kotersky's "Mature Adult Member of the Species."
37 10-24-92 "Learning a Continuous Family Responsibility, Calvin Coolidge High School, Washington, D.C.; by interpretation this is also alluded to in 23: 12-14.
38 Untitled transcript "Darsul Fajr Project."

giving to the human soul of something from the
Nafs of G-d.[39]

Another distinguishing feature of the original human
nature, which gives it a unique place within the total
system of creation, is its freedom as compared to all other
forms of life. The Imam says,

> The human nature is not designed like ordinary
> life in nature. Ordinary life is clocked. It's fixed it
> can't change (i.e., its nature), everything bird, bees,
> everything. Their life is fixed. We don't have to
> worry about them corrupting the earth. They can't.
> Their life is fixed. We don't have to even worry
> about one species taking over the others. That's also
> fixed. When one becomes so many something else
> happens to check it. They can't destroy themselves.
> They can't destroy other things unless Allah allows
> it. If they start to get out of balance, there is
> something to check it, then the balance is restored.
> It's clocked. It's balanced. It happens automatically,
> clocked by Almighty G'd. But the human being,
> nothing checks him except his own good nature,
> if he ignores his own good nature he can become
> anything.[40]

---

39 7-5-98 "Faith and Devotion to Family: A Better Life Is Near,"
Harvey, Illinois. This is the mystery of life and consciousness that
the materialist can't fathom and won't accept.
40 4-4-78 "Christ, Water, Jonah, Whale"; Community Night
Chicago, IL.

So, the place of the original human nature in the total system of creation is as the metaphorical head on the body of the universe.

SECTION 3:
QADARA

HOW DOES "OUR CREATED SELF AND NATURE" PROGRESS FROM SIMPLE TO COMPLEX?

THE DIVINE TRUTH ABOUT EVOLUTION

BEFORE ELABORATING ON a particular quote on the growth of human consciousness from the Imam, I need to dispel prevailing misconceptions about evolution—especially as it is promoted in western society.

As Allah says in The Holy Quran 23:12

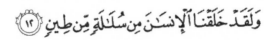

"Verily, We created man from a quintessence of clay;"

This verse is a very explicit statement about the origins of man on earth. Or should we say, "from the earth"?

Like many of my peers, I tacitly rejected the notion of evolution because of what had been popularized and attributed to it. What we rejected about Darwinian evolution was the "from-monkey-to-man" version of evolution. Nevertheless, there is no shortage of support for, nor is there any explicit denial of, evolution as one of the mechanism by which Allah realizes his plan.

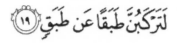

84:19. You shall surely travel from stage to stage.

Darwinian evolution, as promoted by the elite in this society as proof that the creation has "no G'd given purpose," is a lie. Even so, there is truth in the scientific observations drawn out by Darwin. Imam Mohammed expresses his opposition to popular thoughts on Darwinian evolution with balance. Opposing the popular role and view of Darwin's theory, he said,

> This is the society where Darwin's law is holy and sacred; "the survival of the fittest". They're gonna' make sure the character of the society always remains that; that it remains a test for "the survival of the fittest." So, they have to keep it that way. Because they think it's the natural order for man.

> But immorality, injustice, cruelty, homosexuality, perversion, drugs, and liquor problems, these things are not accidental (i.e., though popular Darwin's Theory proposes that random mutation—accidents—as the rule of nature). But if they're accidental (random) then how come

certain societies are not having these accidents.[41]
The truth is that somebody is feeding these things
in western society to keep it burdened. So the
process of elimination continues.[42]

Affirming some of the implications of Darwinian theory,
the Imam said,

> I agree with Darwin, in part. This physical image
> and likeness (our human bodies) belongs to the
> animal kingdom. Although, there is something
> special about our physical symmetry and our design
> . . . that makes us the top of the animal kingdom.
> . . . *Man needs the physical to exist, for communi-*
> *cation, for his existence in this world. However, he is*
> *a spiritual entity. Man is a spiritual entity. Man is to*
> *be understood in the abstract (mental, spiritual) not*
> *in the concrete (the biological), he is to be known and*
> *identified in the abstract[43] not in the concrete.[44]*

How the Original Humanity Gets from "Nowhere" to "Now Here"

We have stated that our original created nature was
conceived by Allah in a realm above and beyond all
categories of thought with which we humans are familiar.
It is a domain that could be seen as "Nowhere." In fact, the
Quran says there was a time when man was "No-thing."

41 Add the commentary on Random Selection as false here.
42 11-25-90 "Family Concerns," Los Angeles, CA.
43 That is in "The Pattern, The Spirit, The Intention of Allah, The
Inherent Will"
44 8-14-93 Imam W. D. Mohammed, Interview Milwaukee,
Wisconsin.

هَلْ أَتَىٰ عَلَى ٱلْإِنسَـٰنِ حِينٌ مِّنَ ٱلدَّهْرِ لَمْ يَكُن شَيْئًا مَّذْكُورًا ۝

76:1. Has there not been over Man a long period of Time when he was nothing— (not even) mentioned?

But then Allah "conceived the human being" and gave him his first existence; Allah set his human creation on its sacred journey toward full expression in space and time. The sacred journey of our original created self and nature begins in the matter of the universe and continues in the earth. Imam Mohammed (ra) explains the earthly portion of our sacred journey in the following quote. He said,

> . . . God raises us up. He creates us in this earth. Our physical essences are of this creation, of this earth—in this physical universe. Our conscience is born of this physical environment, this natural environment. And God has already set the pattern of that growth, that progress, in the physical matter that we are from—and, also, in our biology, and, also, in the spiritual makeup that lives in this biology.[45] It all connects brothers and sisters.

The physical matter has the pattern. That pattern comes into me and I become a living being. That pattern is now in me as a physical living being. The pattern is in my physiology, now it reaches

---

45 *Transduction* is the action or process of converting something and especially energy or a message into another form. Transduction is important here and connects with 56:60-65; Life from "nothing" is a kind of Transduction and Death from Life is also a form of Transduction.

my mental make-up, my conscience. And, now, it begins to set the pattern of my conscience.[46] God has designed all of this!! And it brings us up step by step. We become a part of a social order, living and interacting with each other.

And, the influences that we exert on each other affect the way that we conform to that pattern that Allah has set our creation upon. The Holy Qur'an—chapter 30, verse 30, tells us that in a very few words and very clearly. It tells us that ' God has created the human being on that pattern that he has established the universe on.' And on that same pattern which he has patterned, he has placed the religion upon. The religion coincides with the pattern. The religion is just a higher expression or a revelation of that same pattern. And that is the life we must live.[47] So, the outward life we live is told internally.[48]

When the Imam states that *"The physical matter has the pattern,"* he is also stating that the *Qadr* (the potential and the destiny) is a part of our being. At first, it's there "latent and unrealized." When the Imam states that *"That pattern comes into me and I become a living being,"* he is affirming what the Quran says about our human evolution, physically and abstractly in Chapter 23: 12-14.

46 See https://www.youtube.com/watch?v=HL45pVdsRvE (Capuchin Monkeys Cucumbers and Grapes). It speaks to Virtue and Values (e.g., fairness, justice, etc.) in nature.
47 See "Source Code and Object Code," Commentary Appendix the referenced document.
48 Imam W. D. Mohammed, "The Growth of Human Consciousness."

23: 12. Man We did create from a quintessence (of clay);

13. Then We placed him as (a drop of) sperm in a place of rest firmly fixed;

14. Then We made the sperm into a clot of congealed blood; then of that clot We made a (fetus) lump; then We made out of that lump bones and clothed the bones with flesh; then We developed out of it another creature: so blessed be Allah the Best to create!

In this particular line of reasoning, man, as mentioned in verse 12, is synonymous with "the pattern" and its genesis in 3-dimensional space. In the 14th verse, the Quran reveals the point at which the evolving pattern emerges from the physiology (organic matter). It says, "then We developed out of it another creature."

The verb that Allah uses to describe how he brings about "another creature" is *Na-shaa-a, meaning* "produced; originate; to cause to rise." It has a root *masdar,* meaning "of what has sprouted up but has not become thick, the place of the origination of anything, the first part of the night and of the day, rising after sleeping."[49] Each of these meanings implies that this is the point at which the original nature is just beginning its "spiritual existence in this world/realm."

Imam Mohammed states that "Spirit is the urge in us promoting growth in accordance with Allah's Will."[50] This "Spirit" is another name for "another creature." It names

49 Lane's Lexicon p. 2791.
50 Imam Mohammed (ra) "Family and Progress," Newark, NJ 7/30/95.

54

our original created self and nature. Like a "birdie" in an egg trying to peck its way out of the shell which has been its home and womb since inception, the "Spirit" with its destiny from Allah, has been pushing to come out of matter into this domain of earthly space and time and express itself as "human consciousness."

The modern activist, atheist theory of evolution posits no purpose, no plan, no aim, no creative intelligence, no G'd's Will and no G'd—only "selfish genes as the cause of human creation. On the contrary, it has been the Will of Allah in the form of the urge for progress and development toward more and more excellence in form and performance that has been moving creation forward, especially the human creation.

The Imam states that, "now it reaches my mental make-up, my conscience. And, now, it begins to set the pattern of my conscience." In this, he's describing the effects of this "another creature" arriving at the stage of human mental evolution. Up to this point, I have used the original quote that I received in the transcription of "The Growth of Human Consciousness." However, I am of the strong opinion that the Imam didn't actually use the term *conscience* twice in this section of his commentary. In his public address in Newark, New Jersey, July 30, 1995, he spelled the word *W-O-R-K* and went on to explain why he did that. He said that sometimes the transcribers err and fail to edit his lectures based on the flow of the idea that the Imam may be addressing. Thus, I think the flow of the idea and the subject matter warrant the following adjustment: "Now it reaches my mental make-up, my conscious [mind]. And, now, it begins to set the pattern of my conscience."

Why? The reason is that the extracted quote is addressing the evolution of our original nature, stage by stage. At this point in the quote, it is addressing the arrival of that nature to the level of the mind (mental makeup). The mental makeup is the conscious mind or consciousness (which is actually in the received title). Furthermore, the Imam is speaking of the influence of that nature on the "now living person/conscious person" and how "it begins to set the pattern of my conscience" (i.e., my perception of right and wrong).

While a person can be conscious without a conscience, a person can't have a conscience without being conscious. So, the Imam is saying that when that original created nature dawns at the mental level, it makes the person "conscious," and then it begins to shape their "conscience," their sense of right and wrong. I have found more direct support for this position from the Imam's publication, "Thoughts for Searchers," when he's addressing, essentially, the same subject.

In that publication, he addresses the *Khalifah* and our development as human beings. He said, "It is called the ganglia that, that comes from the spine to the brain and goes back down, back into the system, back into the whole body. It comes into the conscious, sometimes, maybe no time."[51] What "comes into the conscious, sometimes, maybe no time" is a person's awareness of their own original human nature. Failure to "be blessed" with that

---

51 Imam W. D. Mohammed "Thoughts for Searchers," pp. 13-15.

awareness/consciousness precludes that original human nature from beginning to "shape their conscience."

The Imam further states that, "So it [original human nature] goes from the ganglia to the forebrain most of the time it comes *there but it doesn't register to the conscious.*" The message is that "were it to register to the conscious," it would begin to "shape their conscience. Furthermore, the Imam said, "So it [Khalifah consciousness/original human nature] can come up to the brain *(neurological matter)* and the brain can release it to the conscious *(mental make-up and subsequent "conscience")* if the person is conditioned to bring it out; and you know that's what Khalifah is. Khalifah means, "that that is behind you" *[in your evolutionary past].* Finally, he said, "So G'd made Khalifah and G'd made Adam, The Khalifah. It means that *He made Adam to register his past in his consci*ous."

So, there are at least five major ways that this "pattern" and "another creature" can be identified:

1. Spirit: Spirit can be read as synonymous to "the pattern." For example, for the sake of the flow of the idea in the new sentence, I'm adding some particles of speech. The physical matter has the "Spirit." (When) that "Spirit" comes into me (then) I become a living being. (Before that occurs) that "Spirit" is (already) in me as a physical living being. The "Spirit" is in my physiology. Now (when) it reaches my mental make-up, my conscious, (that) "Spirit" begins to (shape) my conscience.

2. The intention of Allah for my created self and nature: This phrase can also be read as synonymous

to "the pattern." For example, "the physical matter has the "The intention of Allah for my created self and nature." That intention of Allah for my created self and nature comes into me, and I become a living being. That intention of Allah for my created self and nature is now in me as a physical living being. The intention of Allah for my created self and nature is in my physiology; now it reaches my mental makeup, my conscious. And, now, the intention of Allah for my created self and nature begins to operate in my conscience.

3. Imam Mohammed (ra) said also, "every man is given by his Gd; excellence of creation, honorable creation and noble birth. And we have an inherent will that the world did not give us. There is a will in us that Gd created us with." [52] That inherent will is also synonymous with "The Pattern, The Spirit, and The intention of Allah for my created self and nature."

4. Inherent Will: Inherent Will can also be read as synonymous to "the pattern." For example, the physical matter has the "inherent will." That inherent will comes into me, and I become a living being. That inherent will is now in me as a physical living being. The inherent will is in my physiology; now it reaches my mental makeup, my *conscious*. And, now, the inherent will begins to shape my conscience.

---

52 W.D Mohammed, "Justice in Islam: How Close Are We Muslims to Western Democracy," *Muslim Journal.* June 6, 2001.

5. Khalifah Consciousness: Khalifah Consciousness can also be read as synonymous to "the pattern." For example, the physical matter has Khalifah consciousness. [When] that Khalifah consciousness comes into me [then] I become a living being. [Before that occurs] that "Khalifah Consciousness" is [already, as a potential] in me as a physical living being (i.e., in my matter). The "Khalifah Consciousness" is in my physiology. Now [when] it reaches my mental make-up, my conscious, [that] "Khalifah Consciousness" begins to [shape] my conscience.

The Original Human Nature Was as a Seed Planted in the Matter of the Earth

Another key verse in the Holy Quran, which reinforces the fact that we are evolutionary creatures is the 17th verse of the 71st Chapter Nuh (Noah). It states,

$$وَٱللَّهُ أَنۢبَتَكُم مِّنَ ٱلْأَرْضِ نَبَاتًا ﴿١٧﴾$$

71: 17.[53] "And Allah has produced you from the earth growing (gradually).

This verse also expresses our origin as an evolutionary being from the matter of the earth.[54] When we read this

---

53 The palindrome insight in this verse actually contains the entire message of the movement from concrete to abstract, our evolution to "sacred maturity" whereby the endowment of our nature becomes fully expressed in this life.
54 23:12–14 as well. Verse 12 "from a quintessence of clay." Also v. 14 Na-shaa-a (Produced) carries the meaning of "what has sprouted up but has not become thick" in reference to "another creature." It is the point at which the original nature is just

verse, we can extract two meanings, one literal and the other figurative.

1. "And Allah has produced you from the earth growing (gradually)" – The literal meaning is that Allah has evolved our original humanity (body and nature) out of the earth.

2. "From the earth growing (gradually)" – Taking "the earth" as symbolic, it represents our anatomy and taking "the earth," figuratively, it stands for society." So, the meaning is that Allah has evolved us as *An-Nas*, a social creature, by the dynamic influences arising from the relationship of nature and nurture and by the interface and the mutual interactions between human beings within the society.[55]

This fits neatly into the core quotation from the Imam's *"The Growth of Human Consciousness."* The Imam said, "We become a part of a social order, living and interacting with each other... the influences that we exert on each other affect the way that we conform to that pattern that Allah has set our creation upon."[56]

At this stage of our human evolution (2:36), this "another creature" exerts a mutually influencing social force—each

beginning its "spiritual existence in this world/realm." https://app.box.com/s/l6pn8jy6x6av4i0y8carkh3c9vvf5ums ("From Photosynthesis to Homo-Erectus" Tom Chi).
55   This can be derived from Sura 4 Ayah 1; Sura 17 Ayah 84 as well as Sura 49 Ayah 13 http://www.allamaiqbal.com/publications/journals/review/oct61/5.htm.
56   https://app.box.com/s/auhujcx4z7bbjk7ozf15x3l8pq0ifmgi (Peterson Video "Revealed Morality in Our Human Biology").

of us upon the other (Sura 103). In the social domain, it is like the universal field of gravity in the cosmos. This force, which shapes the human society, emanates from our natural human conscience and from the nature of the social environment (17:84). Our natural human conscience prescribes a kind of natural morality, which is an "expectation written into our human nature by the creator." Human groupings naturally and intuitively (spiritually) embrace these values, and consequently these innate values exert a social force on everyone in the group as well.

The natural human conscience is an expression of Allah's Will in the human being (91:7-10). The social influences are part and parcel of the societies in which we live. But every society's social values are not aligned with the natural human conscience. Nevertheless, social influences impact our human growth and evolution.

There is further bearing for this stage of our human evolution in the following verses of the Holy Qur'an:

Chapter 95. Tin – The Fig

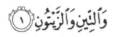

1. By the Fig and the Olive

2. And the Mount of Sinai

وَهَٰذَا ٱلْبَلَدِ ٱلْأَمِينِ ٣

3. And this City of security

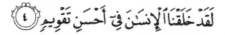

4. We have indeed created man in the best of molds

ثُمَّ رَدَدْنَٰهُ أَسْفَلَ سَٰفِلِينَ ٥

5. Then do We abase him (to be) the lowest of the low

The first three verses of Sura 95 are also revealing evolutionary stages of the original human being.[57] The fourth verse speaks of the "perfection of the original human nature." The fifth verse, however, reminds us that some who are created with that original nature don't achieve it in consciousness or in conscience. And so, they "fall to the lowest of the low." One of the reasons that a person may fall to the "lowest of the low" is because an individual "unblessed" with that awareness/consciousness inhibits their original human nature from "shaping their (social) conscience" in accordance with the Will of Allah.

THE SPIRIT OF MAN AND THE SPIRIT OF ALLAH

The blessed individual has two births/two breaths.

---

57 Fig (ideas, **FIG**urative knowledge) Olive (Ideology, the coherent logic of ideas); Mount Sinai (Divine Revelation/ Inspiration received after Sacred Maturity).

G'd created us to be born just like animals of the womb that are tied to the mother by the Navel Cord, umbilical cord. In the first awakening that we have as human beings we are tied to mother and that is a sign of how we are tied to mother nature. But we got tied to our mother while we were in her. We're tied to mother nature the way we are tied to our mothers that gave birth to us and we can't have life except from her body while we're in her body. Likewise, those who are still under the grip of nature (*i.e., living their lives unconsciously*) and have not awakened to G'd's plan for human beings, they are tied to the Naval Cord of mother nature. And they cannot get any life except from the material world and its nature, G'd has to reveal to them. And like the new baby has to be separated and then take in the breath outside of its mother, we have to be separated from this dependency on natural life and the natural world to latch on to G'd; to take on, to grab a new cord (*i.e., living consciously in accordance with Allah's plan for human life*). The new cord is not flesh and blood the new cord is the Spirit of G'd that comes down from high and connects us to him so we can feed on divine and open up our minds and souls and hearts to a new reality and follow the best of his servants. Isn't it wonderful? G'd has done that for us so let us wake up and respect what he has done for us.[58]

---

58 "Support for Social Dignity and Community Empowerment," pp. 10–11.

Allah reveals the connection between the First Spirit, "natural human conscience from the womb," and the Second Spirit, "inspired human conscience," in the 17th Chapter and the 84th and 85th Verses of the Holy Qur'an. The proximity of these two consecutive verses is a part of the revelation.

قُل كُلٌّ يَعْمَلُ عَلَىٰ شَاكِلَتِهِۦ فَرَبُّكُمْ أَعْلَمُ بِمَنْ هُوَ أَهْدَىٰ سَبِيلًا ۝

17: 84. Says: "Everyone acts according to his own disposition: but your Lord knows best who it is that is best guided on the Way."

وَيَسْـَٔلُونَكَ عَنِ ٱلرُّوحِ قُلِ ٱلرُّوحُ مِنْ أَمْرِ رَبِّى وَمَآ أُوتِيتُم مِّنَ ٱلْعِلْمِ إِلَّا قَلِيلًا ۝

85. They ask thee concerning the Spirit (of inspiration). Say: "The Spirit (cometh) by command of my Lord: of knowledge it is only a little that is communicated to you (O men!)."

17: 84. Is addressing man's First Spirit. That is, man's first spirit which comes from his socialization. Imam Mohammed's statement about the umbilical cord and biological dependence, equates with man's socialization and with man first being more inclined to an unconscious, instinctual "animal existence" or "habit life."

17: 85. Is addressing "The Spirit of/from Allah," the Second Spirit. Imam Mohammed's statement about "the new cord is the Spirit of G'd that comes down from high and connects us to him, . . . " equates with Allah's inspiration coming by his command.

Imam Mohammed sums up the substance in these two verses with this illustration: "The baby comes here with its soul, its inborn sensitivities, and the environment influences its sensitivities, right? And the baby takes on the soul of the world (17: 84 first spirit/first breath), but if we know what God intended for the intellect then we can structure the soul, the conscious, in a way to bring it in agreement with what God has intended for the soul (17: 85 second spirit/second breath)."[59]

The earth, in the Holy Qur'an 71: 17, is symbolic of our anatomy and also of society. "Growing gradually from the earth" means that Allah has evolved us as *An-Nas*, a social creature and as a civilization, by the dynamic influences arising from the relationship of human nature (innate) and nurture (social influences) and by their mutual impact on our human growth and evolution.[60]

The message in the Holy Qur'an 71: 17 connects with the Holy Qur'an 91: 7-10 particularly in verse 9:

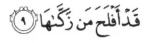

"He is indeed successful who causes it to grow,"

---

59 Imams' Meeting, February 12, 1983, Dallas, Texas.
60 This can be derived from Sura 4 Ayah 1; Sura 17 Ayah 84 as well as Sura 49 Ayah 13

http://www.allamaiqbal.com/publications/journals/review/oct61/5.htm.

The term in the verse is *aflaha* from *falah* (to cultivate). Farmers in the Arabic language are called *Falahin*. They cultivate growth from the earth. Likewise, we have to cultivate the growth of our own soul that has been planted in our matter.

So, Allah planted our Fitrah in the material creation[61] and began the growth of that original humanity on this earthly plane through the interplay of our bodies with the natural environment and with other human beings in society. This is how that original created nature evolves from simple to complex.

---

61 See "Quintessence of Clay" 23: 12-14.

SECTION 4:
HAADA

What is the Role of the Original Human Nature in the Guidance of Allah?

THERE IS A message and guidance in everything that Allah created, including the human being.

إِنَّ فِي ٱخْتِلَٰفِ ٱلَّيْلِ وَٱلنَّهَارِ وَمَا خَلَقَ ٱللَّهُ فِي ٱلسَّمَٰوَٰتِ وَٱلْأَرْضِ لَآيَٰتٍ لِّقَوْمٍ يَتَّقُونَ ٦

Verily in the alternation of the Night and the Day and in all that Allah hath created in the heavens and the earth are Signs for those who fear Him."
(10: 6)

$$\text{سَنُرِيهِمْ ءَايَٰتِنَا فِى ٱلْءَافَاقِ وَفِىٓ أَنفُسِهِمْ حَتَّىٰ يَتَبَيَّنَ لَهُمْ أَنَّهُ ٱلْحَقُّ أَوَلَمْ يَكْفِ بِرَبِّكَ أَنَّهُۥ عَلَىٰ كُلِّ شَىْءٍ شَهِيدٌ ٥٣}$$

"We will show them Our signs in the horizons and within themselves until it becomes clear to them that it is the truth. But is it not sufficient concerning your Lord that He is, over all things, a Witness?" (41: 53)

Imam Mohammed says, "Allah made everything outside of us a language. Everything is a concept. Every concept is a complete message. Everything God created is a complete message. This creation is the writing of God. For example, Stone is negative. It is fixed. (Conceptually) a Stone is (i.e., means) dead to influence."[62]

Since this premise is true, we can conclude that as a part of universal creation, man himself is also a language and a concept. In man's form and nature is a "Great Message" from the Creator. It is a message that unfolds and reveals itself with man's individual and collective growth and evolution as a human being.

OUR HUMAN FORMS PROVIDE GUIDANCE FROM ALLAH

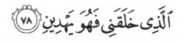

$$\text{ٱلَّذِى خَلَقَنِى فَهُوَ يَهْدِينِ ٧٨}$$

---

62 Imam W. Deen Mohammed, Islamic Studies Class, October 2, 1995.

26: 78. "Who created me and it is He Who guides me;"

According to Wabisah bin Ma'bad, radiyallahu 'anhu, who said: "I came to the Messenger of Allah, sallallahu 'alayhi wasallam, and he said: "You have come to ask about righteousness?" " Yes," I answered. He said: "Consult your heart. Righteousness is that about which the soul feels tranquil and the heart feels tranquil, and sin is what creates restlessness in the soul and moves to and fro in the breast, even though people give you their opinion (in your favor) and continue to do so."

This hadith from Prophet Muhammad (pbuh) confirms what we've stated earlier. Namely, that our natural human conscience prescribes a kind of natural morality, which is a "mutual expectation we have of each other that is written into human nature by the Creator." This natural human conscience is an expression of Allah's Will in the human being, and it acts as a source of guidance for our lives in this world.

Lie detectors depend upon the inherent truthfulness in the nature of human beings. If a human being deviates from making true statements, there is a natural response from the body that conveys the inconsistency. The truth will be in the body, while the lie is in the mind.

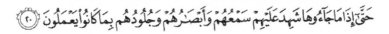

41: 20. At length when they reach the (Fire) their hearing their sight and their skins will bear witness against them as to (all) their deeds.

وَقَالُواْ لِجُلُودِهِمْ لِمَ شَهِدتُّمْ عَلَيْنَا قَالُوٓاْ أَنطَقَنَا ٱللَّهُ ٱلَّذِىٓ أَنطَقَ كُلَّ شَىْءٍ وَهُوَ خَلَقَكُمْ أَوَّلَ مَرَّةٍ وَإِلَيْهِ تُرْجَعُونَ ﴿٢١﴾

41: 21. They will say to their skins: "Why do you bear witness against us?" They will say: "Allah has given us speech; (He) Who gives speech to everything: He created you for the first time and unto Him were ye to return."

These verses also speak to the communicative quality in our physical bodies and in all matter. "Allah gives speech to everything."

Allah's guidance in our form and nature first manifests in the natural urge to improve, to advance, to develop, and to grow.

For the human being, it is as the Imam (ra) has said, the intention of Allah for my created self and nature "begins to operate (in) my conscience." He said also, "every man is given by his Gd; excellence of creation, honorable creation and noble birth. And we have an inherent will that the world did not give us. There is a will in us that Gd created us with."[63]

All matter has the inherent will. And the entire cosmos projects that inherent will as a message from the Creator. The entire universe is communicating Allah's intention for creation, including and especially Allah's intention for the human being." When the human being is blessed to see and hear and understand that message, they become a living being ["another creature", 23: 12-14]. When that

63 W.D Mohammed "Justice in Islam: How Close Are We Muslims to Western Democracy" _ *Muslim Journal.* June 6, 2001.

inherent will moves through their physiology, and reaches their mental makeup, their *consciousness* begins to (shape) their conscience, it becomes a source of guidance. It is by that means that they will attain sacred maturity.

SACRED MATURITY

2: 158 ". . . And if anyone obeys his own impulse to good be sure that Allah is He Who recognizes and knows."

This is the state I call, *sacred maturity*. It is the attainment of that Second Breath, that Second Spirit, when the individual becomes "another creature." With this condition comes our ability to extract knowledge from the cosmos, which provides guidance. Imam Mohammed(ra) said,

"The creation of man is also, more importantly the creation, of a creature that will study G_d's universe and use knowledge."[64]

The attainment of sacred maturity brings the capability to receive guidance from Allah through inspiration.

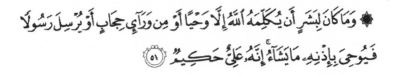

---

64 Ramadan Session 2001, p. 23.

"It is not fitting for a man that Allah should speak to him except by inspiration, or from behind a veil, or by the sending of a messenger to reveal, with Allah's permission, what Allah wills: for He is Most High, Most Wise." (42: 51)

b-1. Wahy – Inspiration by intuition which includes knowledge from deep within yourself and your genetic history all the way back to Adam (what is written in our original nature). By the way, there is significance in the fact that the consonants of the Quranic term for *inspiration* are W (Waw) H (Ha) Y (Yaa) which, without the vowels, transliterate to the English word "Why." This implies that this first form of "G_d's speech to man" (inspiration) comes by man asking "Why?"

b-2. Wara'i Hijabaa – Insight into a matter by inspired intuition or by intellectual processes (ijtihaad, Logic, spiritual literacy, Science, etc.)

b-3. Yursila Rasulan - Muhammad is Allah's Messenger and the Last Prophet. (but not the last messenger. See 33:40)

When the Prophet (pbuh) commissioned Mu'adh Ibn Jabal(ra) as the first governor to Yemen, he asked him

"What will you base your judgment on?"

"According to the Book of God," replied Muadh.

"And if you find nothing therein?"

"According to the Sunnah of the Prophet of God."

"And if you find nothing therein?"

"Then I will exert myself to form my own judgment." The Prophet was pleased with this reply and said:

"Praise be to Allah who has guided THE MESSENGER of the Prophet to that which pleases the Prophet."

$$\text{مَّا كَانَ مُحَمَّدٌ أَبَآ أَحَدٍ مِّن رِّجَالِكُمْ وَلَكِن رَّسُولَ اللَّهِ وَخَاتَمَ النَّبِيِّـنَ ۗ وَكَانَ اللَّهُ بِكُلِّ شَىْءٍ عَلِيمًا ۝}$$

33:40 Muhammad is not the father of [any] one of your men, but [he is] the Messenger of Allah and the last of the prophets. And ever is Allah, of all things, Knowing.

In this verse Muhammad is identified as both Messenger and Prophet, but only identified as the "Last Prophet." W-H-Y didn't Allah say, "the last of the prophets and the last of the messengers?" Isn't there guidance in the fact that the verse itself ends by Allah saying He is "Always knowing everything," telling the reader "Yes, I know you could read what I have revealed as "Allah's Sunnah of sending messengers **hasn't** ended with Muhammad(pbuh). Perhaps that's an understanding that I want to guide the sincere (Mukhlisina Lahuddin) to as well."

Furthermore, the hadith identifies Mu'adh as a "guided messenger."

The last part of that hadith, particularly the third step that Mu'adh replied with, implies arriving at a condition which enables one, with the guidance of Allah, to extract knowledge from their own "Self."

There is also significance in the fact that this verse is numbered 33:40. These numbers invoke Jesus Christ's 33-year mission on the earth and the 40 years of the "first life of Muhammad ibn Abdullah" (10:16) before he received the revelation upon the excellence of his original nature of which Christ is also a symbol. Both Christ and Mohammed (peace be upon the Prophets) understood themselves to be model examples of what is in the potential of all human beings who are sincere in their service to humanity and their worship of G_d.

Jesus Christ:

John 14: 20 "On that day you will realize that I am in my Father, and you are in me, and I am in you."

"The Father" stands for Adam, not G'd. Adam is "the pattern" (see patern-ity) of the original human nature. Jesus is called "The Son of Man" in the Bible. "Adam is Man" in the first reference (Genesis 1: 26-27). The rest of the verse is saying that you and I have the same Father and the same nature.

Prophet Muhammad:

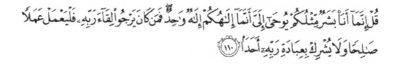

قُلْ إِنَّمَآ أَنَا۠ بَشَرٌ مِّثْلُكُمْ يُوحَىٰٓ إِلَىَّ أَنَّمَآ إِلَٰهُكُمْ إِلَٰهٌ وَٰحِدٌ فَمَن كَانَ يَرْجُوا۟ لِقَآءَ رَبِّهِۦ فَلْيَعْمَلْ عَمَلًا صَٰلِحًا وَلَا يُشْرِكْ بِعِبَادَةِ رَبِّهِۦٓ أَحَدًۢا ۝

Say, "I am only a man like you, to whom has been revealed that your G'd is one G'd. So whoever would hope for the meeting with his Lord - let him do righteous work and not associate in the worship of his Lord anyone."

The point to be made here is that there is still the possibility for a man to be a messenger *[not as one receiving revelation in the manner that Prophet Muhammad (pbuh) received the Holy Qur'an through the agency of the Angel Jibril,]*, but only as one guided by Allah to higher understanding and who takes that understanding as a "message" to people as Mu'adh Ibn Jabal, the guided messenger of The Last Prophet.

32: 7. He Who has made everything which He has created most Good. He began the creation of man with (nothing more than) clay

8. And made his progeny from a quintessence of the nature of a fluid despised:

9. But He fashioned him in due proportion and breathed into him something of His spirit. And He gave you (the faculties of) hearing and sight and feeling (and understanding): little thanks do ye give!

In "Education: A Sacred Matter," the Imam points out that "The universe is communicating to our mind."[65] He says that the patterns and laws in operation in creation

---

65 P.33-34, 51.

are a communication in "the language of the soul."[66] He says that when Adam, our sacred human nature, is "reconciled with the nature created by G_d [Macrocosm], it/he finds those patterns for our thinking[67] which bring us to the great destination[68] that God wants us to reach for our capacity and our potential inside of us.[69]

---

66 "Signs" in creation p.53-54, ***94-95; also ***p. 66 "For Those Who Thirst."
67 2:37 "Adam met words from his Lord"
68 2: 38. We said: "Get ye down all from here; and if as is sure there comes to you guidance from Me" whosoever follows My guidance on them shall be no fear nor shall they grieve.
69 Page 117 "Education: A Sacred Matter."

CONCLUSION

S O IN LIGHT of the question, the answer and the principles laid down by the Imam, I've set before you the answer, and only Allah knows best, to the question "What are the four things we need to know about our "Sacred Self", so that we might "know everything about that thing"? The answer is:

We know our True Form – Our sacred human nature is all of the excellent human qualities and all the human virtues of the masculine and the feminine, as conceived by Allah before they were embodied to our male and female anatomies.

We know our place in the total system of creation – Our sacred human nature is the metaphorical head on the body of the universe.

We know our potential for growth from simple to complex – Our sacred human nature was placed into the material creation by Allah and evolved on the earth through the

79

interplay of our bodies with the natural environment and with other human beings in social settings.

We know our Place in the Guidance of G'd – When Our sacred human nature matures, it gives rise to the capacity to receive Allah's communication from both within ourselves and from the material creation [70]. This maturity enables us to be guided through our own souls in accordance with the Will of Allah.

---

70   10: 31 "Say: «Who is it that sustains you (in life) from the sky and from the earth?"

About the Author
Imam Faheem Shuaibe

FAHEEM SHUAIBE is a thought provoking leader and has been the Resident Imam of Masjidul Waritheen in Oakland, California for 34 years. A lifelong student of Imam W. Deen Mohammed (ra), Imam Faheem's unique ability to take complex ideas and make them relatable has led to him serving as a frequently requested presenter at major national conferences sponsored by non-profit and philanthropic organizations. His lectures address diverse audiences on a wide range of topics including religion, world politics, human relationships and societal evolution.

Over the span of more than 4 decades, Imam Faheem has dedicated his life to the upliftment of humanity. Along with other African American scholars (e.g., Asa Hilliard, Iyanla Van Zant, Dr. Na'im Akbar, et. al.), Imam Faheem Shuaibe has been inducted into the African American Intellectual Royal Family by the Institute for the Advance Study of Black Family Life and Culture. He is also a frequent lecturer at Cal Berkeley's "Holy Hill" for the Graduate Theological Union (GTU) which trains doctoral and post-doctoral students of Philosophy, and Theology.

To address issues he saw around the decline of marriage and family relationships, Imam Faheem founded M.A.R.I.A.M. (Muslim American Research Institute Advocating Marriage) which hosts regular conferences and discussions.

Mr. Shuaibe has also been recognized as a part of several distinguished delegations that have taken him around the globe on various educational, religious, interfaith, and peace missions including Saudi Arabia, Italy, Sudan, Malaysia, Egypt, The British Isles and the Caribbean. Passionate about interfaith relations, Imam Faheem is founding member of an "A list" of intellectuals, professionals, religious leaders and career diplomats on the "Abraham Family Reunion Project."

You may find more of Imam Faheem's lectures and writings on one of his 6 weekly Blog Talk Radio shows under his *A Clear Understanding* Broadcasts: "Wealth Creation and Preservation," "All Things Human," "For those Who Thirst," "Universal Dimensions of Leadership," "The Qur'an Salat Institute," and "Juma'ah Live from Masjidul

Waritheen in Oakland, California." His lectures are also broadcast on aclearunderstanding.net and are a rich source of inspiration and information to students across the country.

He has been married to Yolanda Mahasin Shuaibe for 46 years. They have 4 children and 3 grand-children.

You may reach him at sabilillah@aol.com.

Made in the USA
San Bernardino, CA
15 April 2018